Here is the Which Way crew who will help you wind your way through Iowa:

CHIP wears a baseball cap to protect his delicate circuits. He'll feel right at home at an unusual Iowa baseball field.

Rita Mapp loves the outdoors. She can't wait to see the sights from the basket of a hot-air balloon in Indianola.

Table of Contents

WHO is heading for the WHICH WAY HALL OF FAME?

WHAT will be in the WHICH WAY MUSEUM?

WHERE will the WHICH WAY SUPERMAX MOVIE be filmed?

Trailblazing

Your journey begins in Council Bluffs, Iowa. The city is named for a nearby bluff that overlooks the Missouri River. Explorers Lewis and Clark met here with the Oto Indians and planned their trip west.

The crew members go to the Western Historic Trails Center. As they walked on the granite path toward the museum, they noticed some names written on polished stone slabs. CHIP says that there are nearly 1,000 names. Some are names of pioneers who traveled westward. Others name the Indian nations they met.

According to Professor Pfeffer, the Lewis and Clark Trail is one of several famous Iowa routes. The crew studies the large United States map at the museum entrance. Look at the map pictured here and help the crew figure out how many of these trail tales are true. Then blaze a trail to the bottom of page 3.

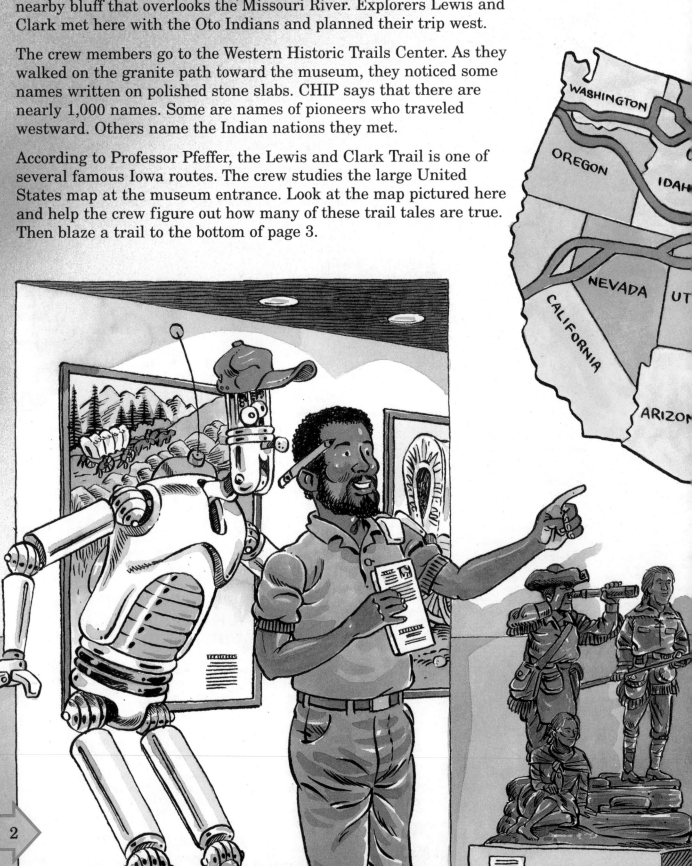

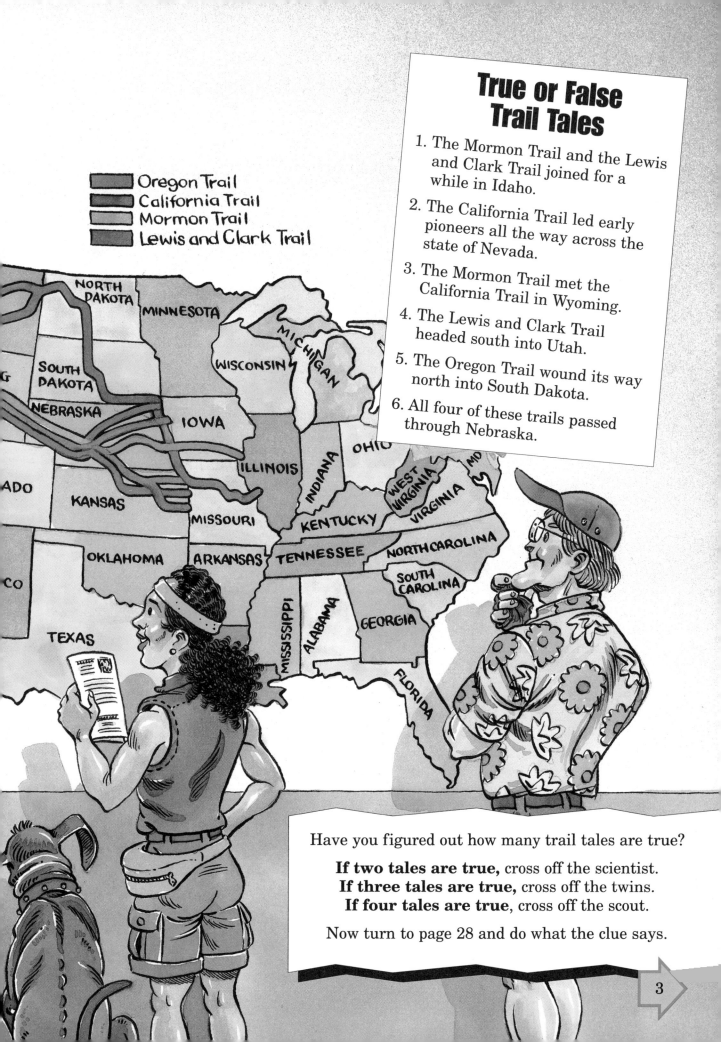

Oregon Trail
California Trail
Mormon Trail
Lewis and Clark Trail

True or False Trail Tales

1. The Mormon Trail and the Lewis and Clark Trail joined for a while in Idaho.

2. The California Trail led early pioneers all the way across the state of Nevada.

3. The Mormon Trail met the California Trail in Wyoming.

4. The Lewis and Clark Trail headed south into Utah.

5. The Oregon Trail wound its way north into South Dakota.

6. All four of these trails passed through Nebraska.

Have you figured out how many trail tales are true?

If two tales are true, cross off the scientist.
If three tales are true, cross off the twins.
If four tales are true, cross off the scout.

Now turn to page 28 and do what the clue says.

A Wild Goose Chase?

The crew piles into the Which Way wheels. Hugh drives north on Interstate 29 to the DeSoto National Wildlife Refuge near Missouri Valley, Iowa. This wetland is important to migrating birds. Each year, as many as 500,000 snow geese may stop here on their way north or south.

Rita takes Baskerville for a walk along the nature trails in this 8,000-acre preserve. Professor Pfeffer grabs his binoculars and joins a group of bird-watchers who are talking about how far they have come to get here. Check your Which Way map to locate where each person came from. Then fly down to the bottom of page 5.

I can't believe I came all the way from Keokuk to see a duck.

There's a lot to do in Cedar Rapids, but more to see in the skies here.

Highlights WHICH WAY USA? STATE MAP

Don't Forget Your Map!
Use your Iowa map to solve this puzzle. You'll need to locate six different places.

4

5

Pass the Popcorn!

The crew heads to Sioux City. After romping through the DeSoto refuge, Baskerville is ready for a snack. The Which Way hound leads the way to the American Popcorn Company. This *pop*-ular company doesn't even have to leave the state for its main ingredient. Corn grows on many of Iowa's 100,000 farms.

The crew takes a special tour of the factory. Then they head to the factory store to sample some popcorn treats. Before you join them, you have some work to do. Unscramble the mixed-up words in this recipe. Write the correct letters in the spaces on page 7. When you're done, pop down to the bottom of the page.

Which Way Popcorn Balls

2 **CSUP** sugar
2/3 cup apple juice or water
2/3 cup **AMPEL** syrup
1/2 cup butter
1 1/2 teaspoons salt
1 teaspoon vanilla
4 quarts warm popped **CROPNOP**
1 cup peanuts
1 1/2 cups chopped dates

Combine sugar, apple **UJICE**, syrup, butter, and salt in a heavy saucepan. Bring to a **LOIB**, stirring occasionally. Remove the **GRAUS** that forms on the sides of the pan with a wet brush. **COKO**, without stirring, until mixture reaches 270°F on a candy thermometer. Stir in vanilla. Pour mixture over popped popcorn, peanuts, and chopped **SADET**. Mix well. **PHESA** the mixture into 3-inch balls.

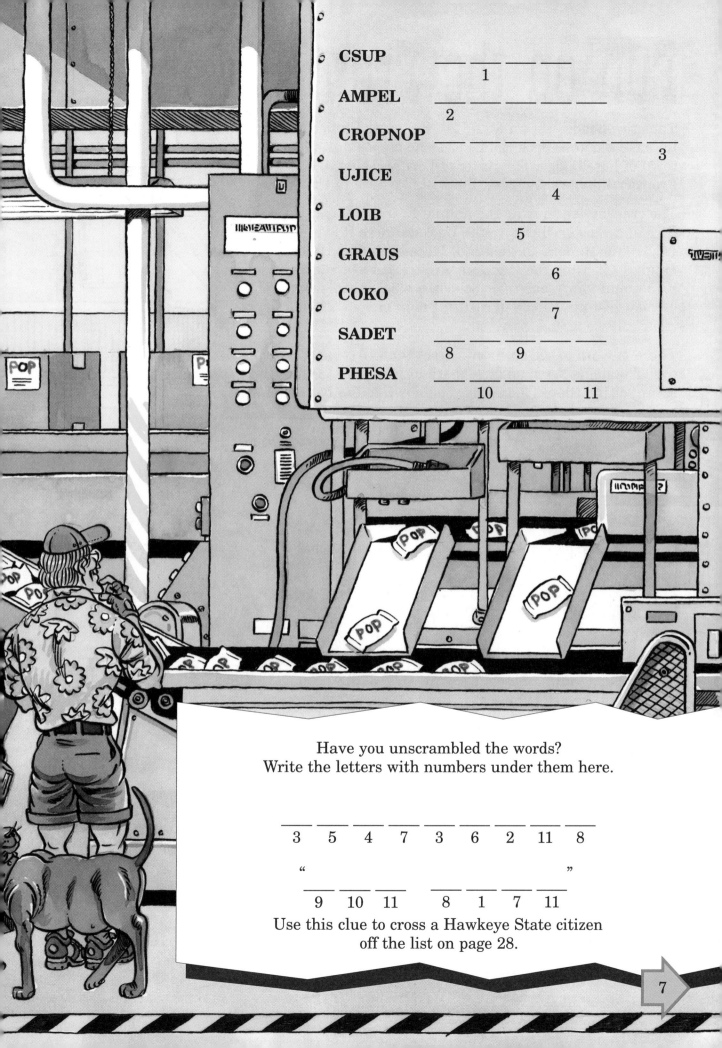

CSUP ___ ___ ___ ___
1

AMPEL ___ ___ ___ ___ ___
2

CROPNOP ___ ___ ___ ___ ___ ___ ___
3

UJICE ___ ___ ___ ___ ___
4

LOIB ___ ___ ___ ___
5

GRAUS ___ ___ ___ ___ ___
6

COKO ___ ___ ___ ___
7

SADET ___ ___ ___ ___ ___
8   9

PHESA ___ ___ ___ ___ ___
10   11

Have you unscrambled the words?
Write the letters with numbers under them here.

___ ___ ___ ___ ___ ___ ___ ___ ___
3   5   4   7   3   6   2   11   8

"___ ___ ___ ___ ___ ___ ___"
9   10   11   8   1   7   11

Use this clue to cross a Hawkeye State citizen
off the list on page 28.

Fun on the Frontier

The crew heads east on Route 20. Professor Pfeffer is eager to make a detour back in history! The crew stops at the town of Fort Dodge. The restored Fort Museum and Frontier Village show what life was like here in the 1850s.

The crew arrives during the annual Frontier Days Festival. Rita and Baskerville go to the Buckskinners Rendezvous, where "fur traders" gather and dance to fiddled tunes. Hugh, CHIP, and the Professor walk down historic Front Street and tour a one-room school, a blacksmith shop, and a general store. People in costume help make the Old West come alive.

There is more to see on Front Street than first meets the eye. The items listed on page 9 are hidden here. Search the scene to find them. Then mosey on down to the bottom of that page.

BLACKSMITH

GENERAL STORE DRY GOODS

GENER

DOG

SNAKE

VASE

MOON

LEMON

JAM

OAR

Have you found all the hidden items?
One of them is hidden twice. Write its
name here:

_____

Look at the letters in the name. Find the
person on page 28 whose full name contains
each of those letters. Cross that
person off your list.

A Fair to Remember

Ready to return to the present, Hugh Tern and the crew steer south toward Des Moines. Iowa's capital and largest city is the site of the Iowa State Fair, which is in full swing. During its eleven-day run, almost one million visitors will stroll through its 160-acre fairgrounds!

Professor Pfeffer, CHIP, and Baskerville take a walk down the midway. Rita and Hugh pick up a fair guide and set out to see the sights. Rita snaps photos of Hugh in eight different places, and they drop off the film to be developed at a one-hour photo place. But when they pick up the pictures, they're all out of order. Thank goodness Rita still has her fair guide! Use it to put the pictures back in order. Then head over to the bottom of page 11.

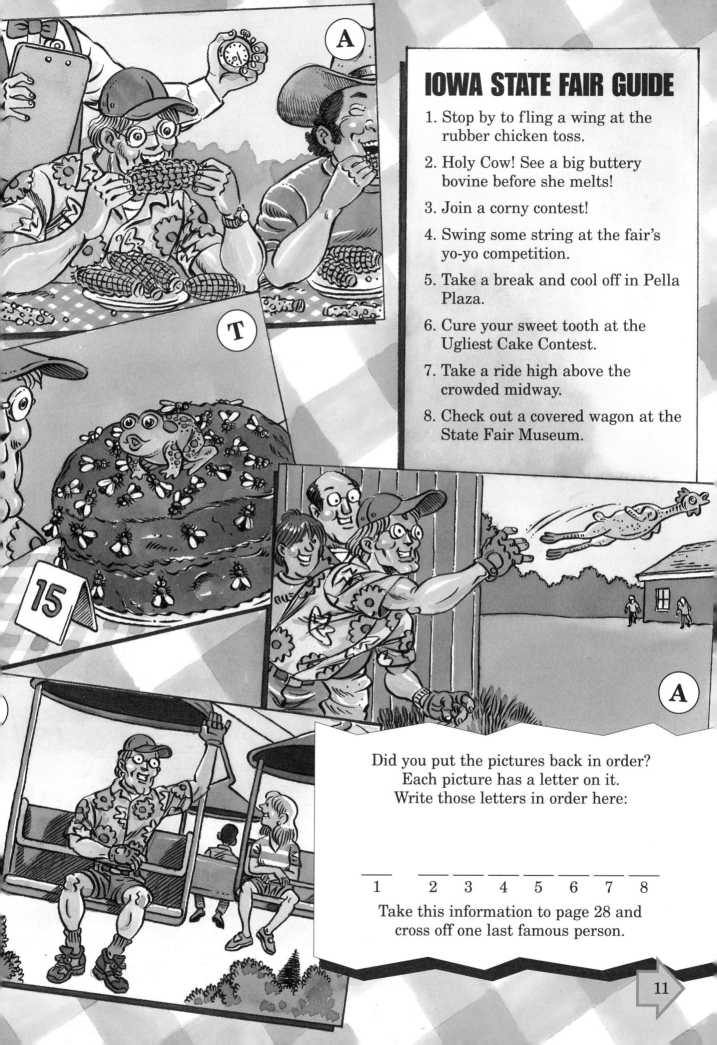

IOWA STATE FAIR GUIDE

1. Stop by to fling a wing at the rubber chicken toss.

2. Holy Cow! See a big buttery bovine before she melts!

3. Join a corny contest!

4. Swing some string at the fair's yo-yo competition.

5. Take a break and cool off in Pella Plaza.

6. Cure your sweet tooth at the Ugliest Cake Contest.

7. Take a ride high above the crowded midway.

8. Check out a covered wagon at the State Fair Museum.

Did you put the pictures back in order?
Each picture has a letter on it.
Write those letters in order here:

___ ___ ___ ___ ___ ___ ___ ___
1   2   3   4   5   6   7   8

Take this information to page 28 and cross off one last famous person.

A Capitol Idea

Before leaving Des Moines, the crew stops by the state capitol building, which is famous for its 23-carat, 275-foot-high, gold-leafed dome. The crew spreads out to go exploring. Hugh dashes up 398 steps to the top of the grand staircase to get a better view of the scale model of the World War II battleship *Iowa*. Baskerville and Rita head outdoors to walk the 165-acre grounds.

Meanwhile, CHIP and the Professor zip over to the towering law library. It's huge, with a 45-foot-high ceiling and about 200,000 books. There they meet a group of students searching out some unusual information about this great state. You can help. Circle the letter of each correct answer. Then look down to the bottom of page 13 for a clue.

Don't Forget Your Map!
The *back* of your map of Iowa contains all the information you need.

1. Which Iowa road is often described as the "crookedest street in the world"?

b. Snake Alley   **c. Boomerang Lane**
d. Zigzag Avenue

2. Which one of these crops does Iowa produce more of than any other state?

a. soy beans   **e. corn**
o. potatoes

12

5. What did Dutch settlers first name Orange City?

    e. Holland   **o. Tulipville**
        u. New Amsterdam

3. Which of these towns was *not* a stop on the Boone & Scenic Valley Railroad?

    r. Ames   **s. Fort Dodge**
        t. Cedar Rapids

6. Which of these contests is *not* featured at the Iowa State Fair?

    r. Donut Juggling
    s. Fastest Grocery Bagger
    t. Bubble Gum Blowing

4. Where can you see the beautiful Nite-Glo Extravaganza?

    h. the Iowa State Fair
    i. the Tulip Festival
    t. the National Balloon Classic

Have you answered all the questions?
Write the letters you circled
in the spaces below.

Your clue is

___ ___ ___ ___ ___ ___.
  1   2   3   4   5   6

Now turn to page 29. Write this code word in the correct spaces.

HIGH Qs?

The crew members next take a quick detour for a train tour! They head northwest to Boone, Iowa, to ride the Boone & Scenic Valley Railroad. Hugh loves the train's steam locomotive. Rita's favorite part is the bird's-eye view of Iowa's "little Grand Canyon," the Des Moines River Valley. She gasps as the train rumbles across the Bass Point Creek Bridge, which is 156 feet above the valley floor.

Professor Pfeffer is filled with facts about this national historic landmark. But CHIP is so excited about the ride, he gets his wires a bit crossed as he inputs the data. A lot of Qs have taken the place of other letters. Replace each Q with the correct letter. When you are finished, steam over to the bottom of page 15.

ON THE RIGHT TRACK?

The Boone & ScenQc Valley Railroad Qirst began in 18[ ] as a coal railwaQ. From 1907 to 1955, it carried peoQpl[ ] too, from Boone to Des Moines and Fort Dodge. Today, i[ ] poQlled by a Qteam locomotive made for it in Daton[ ] China. Its Bass Point Creek Bridge is the highesQ[ ] interurban rQilroad bQidge in NorQh America[ ]

Have you figured out which letters should replace the Qs
in this printout? Write the letters you used,
in order, in the spaces below.

___ ___   ___ ___ ___ ___   ___ ___ ___ ___ ___

Now write these words in the correct spaces on page 29.

Up, Up, and Away

After the train ride ends, the crew returns to the highway. Hugh drives south back through Des Moines. He continues on to Indianola. Rita is ready for a different kind of ride—one in a hot-air balloon. Every summer, this Iowa town is the site of the National Balloon Classic. Rita and the others arrive around dusk. They are just in time to catch the night launch of dozens of hot-air balloons.

Each team member chooses a different balloon basket—even Baskerville! Their balloons glow in the dark as they're waiting to rise. Some clues seem about to burst forth here, too. Calculate the number described on each balloon. There must be a code! CHIP figures that each answer is the same as how high each crew member will fly. After you calculate which two balloons will soar the highest, float over to the clue on the bottom of page 17.

The number of hours i a week X the number c sides on a triangle

The number of stars on an American flag X the number of stripes on the flag

The number of ounces in a pound X the number of minutes in a half hour

The number of pennies in 8 quarters X the number in a trio

The number of days in a leap year + the number of minutes in 4 hours

Did you discover how high each crew member will fly? Use that information to find the correct clue below.

If Hugh and CHIP will fly highest, the word is WITH.
If Rita and Baskerville will, the word is LAST.
If Professor Pfeffer and Hugh will, it is WHEN.
If CHIP and Baskerville will, it is WOOF.

Write the correct code word in the spaces on page 29.

DUTCH TREAT

Hugh steers east for a stop in Pella—or is it Holland? The town has windmills, wooden shoes, and acres of tulips. The crew especially likes the town's musical, animated Klokkenspel. This clock in the town square has figures that dance on the hour, every hour.

Baskerville can't resist chasing a butterfly through a field of colorful tulips. Hugh races after Baskerville and finally catches up to the pesky pooch. But Hugh's sense of direction has left him completely confused. Help him tiptoe through the tulips back to the rest of the crew. After you do, sniff out a clue on the bottom of page 19.

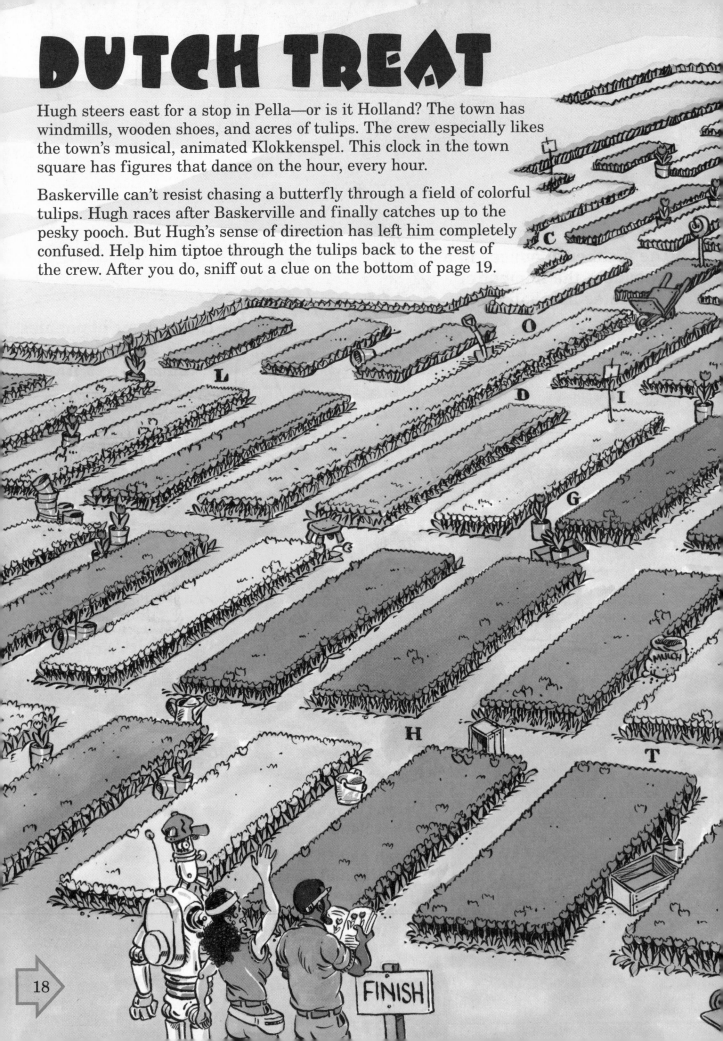

Did you help Hugh find his way from Start to Finish?
Now fill in the spaces below with the letters you passed.

On page 29, write ____ ____ ____ ____ in the correct spaces.

Then shade in the areas in the drawing that
have any letters in the word

____ ____ ____.

A Crafty Code

Professor Pfeffer is eager to explore the Amana Colonies. This is a group of seven villages called Amana, East, West, South, High, Homestead, and Middle. They were founded in the 1800s by artisans and craftsmen. Even today, Amana's artists are world famous. They create some of the most beautiful baskets, blankets, rugs, and furniture in the nation.

The crew stops by the Amana General Store. There are all kinds of handmade objects for sale. The crew members take a closer look at all the things the artists have made. While they discover the secret of these craftspeople, you can uncover a secret, too. Use the pictures to fill in the code on page 21. Then check the box on the bottom of the page.

Did you crack the code? Read the message and then turn to page 30. Use this information to cross off two famous places.

Who but Hoover?

With Hugh at the wheel, the crew heads southeast to West Branch, home of the Herbert Hoover Presidential Library, Museum, and Historic Site. Rita wonders how Hoover's family fit into the 14-by-20-foot cottage in which our 31st president was born. Also on the site are a one-room schoolhouse and 76 acres of tall-grass prairie.

The crew explores the Hoover Museum. Before you join them, you have something to do "first." Find the answers to the famous firsts in Iowa listed on page 23. Use the words in the box below, being sure to cross off each word as you use it. When you are done with your firsts, you have one last thing to do. Check the bottom of page 23.

WORD BOX

JULIEN FORT DES MARS CROSS
LE MOINES OUT RED DUBUQUE
DAVENPORT HERBERT ELK APPLE
MADISON DELICIOUS HORN HOOVER
BATHTUB WINDMILL RACES

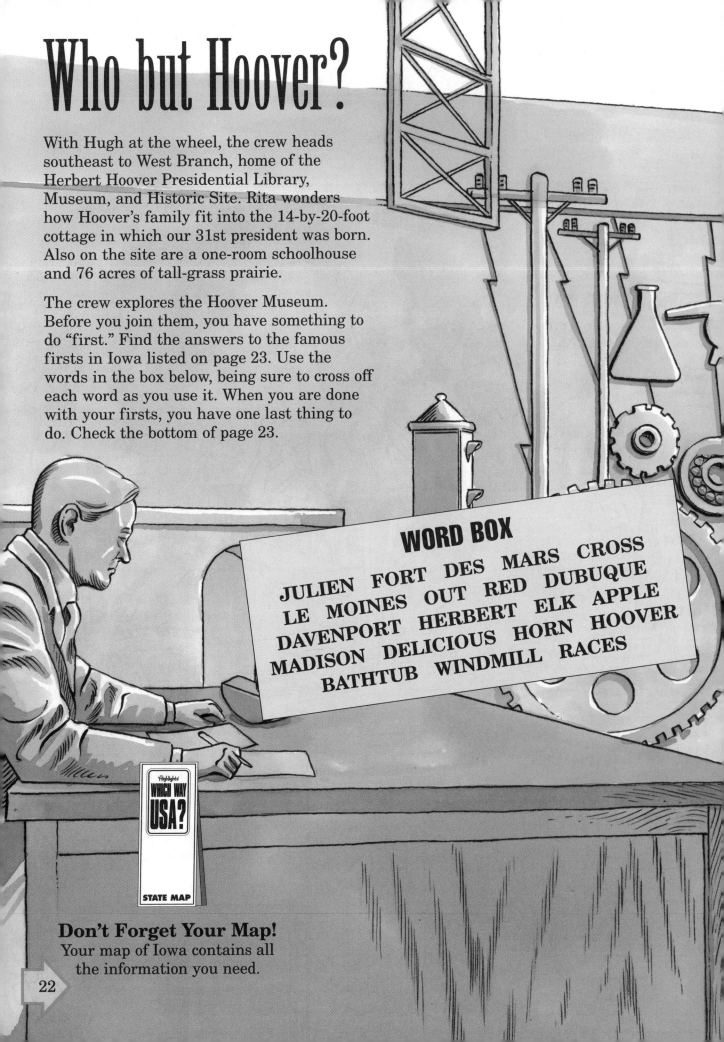

Highlights
WHICH WAY
USA?

STATE MAP

Don't Forget Your Map!
Your map of Iowa contains all
the information you need.

IOWA FIRSTS

1. Iowa's first white settler with a city named for him: _____ _____

2. Top-selling Iowa fruit first named "Hawkeye": _____ _____ _____

3. Indianola event with wet first-place contestants: _____ _____

4. Iowa city spelled with the first letters of six women's names: _____ _____

5. Iowa's first military outpost: _____ _____

6. Iowa city where the first bridge spanning the Mississippi starts (or ends): _____

7. The Iowa city that is first in population: _____ _____

8. Elected in 1928, first president born west of the Mississippi River: _____ _____

WHO BUT HOOVER?

IOWA YOU MAKE ME SMILE

Did you find all the Iowa firsts?
Some of the words in the box are left over. Write those
words, in order from top to bottom, on the lines below.

_____ _____

_____ _____ _____ .

Now do this on page 30.

Cornball?

Hugh drives north. The crew cruises past mile after mile of rich farmland. Finally, the crew members arrive in Dyersville. Among the farms, they find a famous clearing. It's the site where the movie *Field of Dreams* was filmed— a 93-year-old farmhouse with a baseball diamond carved out in a cornfield.

CHIP flips when he sees the diamond. He begins to toss a ball with Rita. Baskerville and Hugh run the bases just for fun. Meanwhile, Professor Pfeffer is working on a list of team names. Included are the Iowa Cubs and some other minor-league baseball teams. Find all the names in the grid on page 25. Circle only the words that are in capital letters. Then swing down to the bottom of the page.

MINOR-LEAGUE BASEBALL TEAMS

Albuquerque **DUKES**
Calgary **CANNONS**
Colorado Springs **SKY SOX**
Edmonton **TRAPPERS**
Fresno **GRIZZLIES**
Iowa **CUBS**
Las Vegas **STARS**
Memphis **REDBIRDS**
Omaha **ROYALS**
Nashville **SOUNDS**
New Orleans **ZEPHYRS**
Oklahoma **REDHAWKS**
Salt Lake **BUZZ**
Tacoma **RAINIERS**
Tucson **SIDEWINDERS**
Vancouver **CANADIANS**

```
S I D E W I N D E R S
N E M S S B U C T X R
A C I U K K U R S O E
I A E L E W A Z U S I
D N M S Z P A O Z Y N
A N U T P Z S H D K I
N O R E D B I R D S A
A N R O O R S R A E R
C S R Y H P E Z G T R
R O Y A L S O U N D S
```

Have you circled the team names?
Now write the leftover letters, from left to
right and top to bottom, here:

___ ___ ___ ___ ___ ___

___ ___ ___ ___ ___ ___ ___ ___

Use this clue to cross out another famous
Iowa landmark on page 30.

Bye-Bye, Iowa!

After running the bases for a final time, CHIP and the crew "slide" into the car. They drive a short way to Dubuque. This city is carved into towering bluffs high above the Mississippi River. Before the crew members say so long to the Hawkeye State, they board *The Spirit of Dubuque*, a sternwheel steamer. They want to finish their journey with a sightseeing cruise down the river.

As they float along, you have one last puzzle to solve. Fill in the answers. Some letters have numbers under them. Write those letters in the spaces on page 27. Then cruise to the bottom of the page.

1. The highest point in Iowa is found in this county.

     __ __ __ __ __ __ __
     1   2

2. Two men from Des Moines built this tasty building.

     __ __ __ __ __ __ __ __ __ __ __   __ __ __ __ __
     3   4

3. These two famous rivers form Iowa's eastern and western borders.

     __ __ __ __ __ __ __ __ __ __ __ and __ __ __ __ __ __ __ __ __
     5   6

4. This Iowa city is near Interstate 80 just across the river from Nebraska.

     __ __ __ __ __ __ __ __ __ __ __ __ __
     7   8   9

5. This city is the state's sixth-largest city and home to the University of Iowa.

     __ __ __ __ __ __ __ __ __
     10   11

6. This is Iowa's state flower.

     __ __ __ __ __ __ __ __
          12   13

WHICH WAY USA?

STATE MAP

Don't Forget Your Map!
The answers can be found on your map of Iowa.

$$\overline{}_{7}\ \overline{}_{13}\ \overline{}_{1}\ \overline{}_{4}\ \overline{}_{4}\qquad \overline{}_{1}\ \overline{}_{9}\qquad \overline{}_{9}$$

$$\overline{}_{2}\ \overline{}_{9}\ \overline{}_{9}\ \overline{}_{10}\ \overline{}_{3}\ \overline{}_{11}\qquad \overline{}_{5}\ \overline{}_{1}\ \overline{}_{6}\ \overline{}_{8}\ \overline{}_{12}\ \overline{}_{4}\,.$$

SPIRIT OF DUBUQUE

PORT OF DUBUQUE

Have you decoded the message? Now turn to page 30 and use this information.

Who?

Which famous Hawkeye Stater will enter the Which Way Hall of Fame? To find out, you need to solve the puzzles on pages 2 through 11. Each puzzle will help you cross someone off the list. When there is only one choice left, he or she is the hall-of-famer!

William Cody
Frontiersman, scout, and marksman, nicknamed "Buffalo Bill," who formed a world-famous Wild West show

Grant Wood
Artist who painted many scenes and people of Iowa, including his most famous work, *American Gothic*

Pauline Esther and Esther Pauline Friedman
Twin sisters who write the popular newspaper advice columns "Dear Abby" and "Ann Landers"

Amelia Jenks Bloomer
Women's rights champion who wore the loose-fitting pants later known as "bloomers"

John Wayne
Actor born Marion Michael Morrison, nicknamed "the Duke," who appeared in more than 175 movies

James Van Allen
Physicist who discovered two radiation belts around Earth that are now called the Van Allen belts

The person going into the Hall of Fame is:

What?

One thing from Iowa will be displayed in the Which Way Museum. To find out what it is, solve the puzzles on pages 12 through 19. Fill in the code words in the correct spaces. The final puzzle will give you a word and also tell you how to shade in the picture.

A Capitol Idea (Pages 12-13): ___ ___ ___ ___ ___
　　　　　　　　　　　　　　　　 1　 2　 3　 4　　 5

High Qs? (Pages 14-15): ___ ___　___ ___　___ ___ ___
　　　　　　　　　　　　 6　 7　　 8　 9　 10　 11　12

Up, Up, and Away (Pages 16-17): ___ ___ ___ ___
　　　　　　　　　　　　　　　　　 13　　 14

Dutch Treat (Pages 18-19): ___ ___ ___ ___
　　　　　　　　　　　　　　 15　 16

Use the second clue from page 19 to shade in the picture.

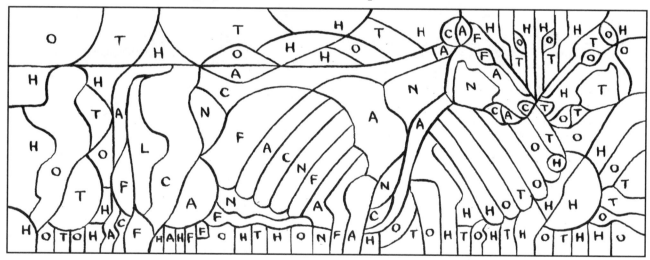

Now write the letters with numbers under them in the spaces below.

The famous item is:

___ ___ ___ ___　___ ___ ___ ___ ___　___ ___ ___ ___
 6　 8　13　11　 10　 3　11　 4　 2　 7　11　 6　 5

___ ___ ___ ___ ___ ___　___ ___ ___
 1　 9　 3　 4　14　12　 15　16　13

Where?

One landmark in Iowa will be part of the Which Way Supermax Movie. To find out where the Which Way cameras will be, solve the puzzles on pages 20 through 27. The puzzles will help you eliminate famous places. When you finish, the remaining landmark is the one you need.

Maquoketa Caves
Underground rock formations, a natural bridge, and 13 limestone caves in an Iowa state park

Elk Horn Windmill
A working 1848 windmill transported from Holland in 30,000 parts

Todd House
Underground Railroad stop in Tabor that has been restored to look as it did before the Civil War

Amana Colonies
Seven villages founded by German settlers, world famous for the work of artists and craftspeople

Living History Farms
Outdoor museum west of Des Moines where visitors "travel" back in time

Effigy Mounds National Monument
Nearly 200 ancient Native American burial mounds, including many shaped like birds and other animals

The famous place is:

All the answers for your
Which Way adventure
are on the next two
pages. Do not go

unless you need help
with a puzzle. If you
don't need help,

before you look at
the answers.

You can use the rest of
this page to work out
your puzzles. If you need
a little extra space,

your pencil here. After
you're done, make a

back to the page you
were working on.

ANSWERS

Pages 2-3: Trailblazing
Three of the tales (#2, #3, and #6) are true. Cross off Pauline Esther Friedman and Esther Pauline Friedman on page 28.

Pages 4-5: A Wild Goose Chase?
Wanda (from Keokuk) and Cecily (from Sioux City) live farthest apart. Since their first initials are **W** and **C**, eliminate **W**illiam **C**ody on page 28.

Pages 6-7: Pass the Popcorn!

<u>C U P S</u>
1

<u>M A P L E</u>
2

<u>P O P C O R N</u>
3

<u>J U I C E</u>
4

<u>B O I L</u>
5

<u>S U G A R</u>
6

<u>C O O K</u>
7

<u>D A T E S</u>
8 9

<u>S H A P E</u>
10 11

<u>N I C K N A M E D</u>   <u>T H E</u>   <u>"D U K E"</u>
3 5 4 7 3 6 2 11 8   9 10 11   8 1 7 11

Cross off John Wayne on page 28.

Pages 8-9: Fun on the Frontier

The vase is hidden twice. Since the letters *V-A-S-E* appear in the name *James Van Allen*, cross him off on page 28.

Pages 10-11: A Fair to Remember
When the pictures are put in order, the letters spell A PAINTER. This eliminates Grant Wood on page 28.

Pages 12-13: A Capitol Idea
1. **b** 2. **e** 3. **t** 4. **t** 5. **e** 6. **r**
The letters of the correct answers spell BETTER. Write this word on page 29.

Pages 14-15: High Qs?
The corrected message reads:

The Boone & Scenic Valley Railroad first began in 1893 as a coal railway. From 1907 to 1955, it carried people, too, from Boone t Des Moines and Fort Dodge. Today, it is pulled by a steam locomotive made for it in Datong, China. Its Bass Point Creek Bridge is the highest interurban railroad bridge in North America.

When the correct letters are substituted in the message, they spell IF YOU START. Write those words in the correct spaces on page 29.

Pages 16-17: Up, Up, and Away
Professor: 50 x 13 = 650
CHIP: (24 x 7) x 3 = 168 x 3 = 504
Baskerville: 16 x 30 = 480
Hugh: 366 + (60 x 4) = 366 + 240 = 606
Rita: (25 x 8) x 3 = 200 x 3 = 600
Professor Pfeffer and Hugh will fly highest so the clue word for page 29 is WHEN.

Pages 18-19: Dutch Treat

The letters on the correct path are C, O, L, D, H, O, and T. Write COLD in the correct spaces. Then shade in all the areas in the picture that have any letters in the word *HOT*. Turn to page 29 and follow these instructions.

Pages 20-21: **A Crafty Code**

The two "underground" sites are Todd House and Maquoketa Caves. Cross them off on page 30.

Pages 22-23: **Who but Hoover?**

1. Julien Dubuque
2. Red Delicious apple
3. bathtub races
4. Le Mars
5. Fort Madison
6. Davenport
7. Des Moines
8. Herbert Hoover

The leftover words say CROSS OUT ELK HORN WINDMILL. Delete this place on page 30.

Pages 24-25: **Cornball?**

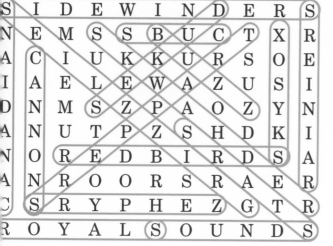

The leftover letters spell MUSEUM OUTDOORS. Cross off the Living History Farms on page 30.

Pages 26-27: **Bye-Bye, Iowa!**

O S C E O L A
1   2

G I N G E R B R E A D   H O U S E
3   4

M I S S I S S I P P I
5

and M I S S O U R I
              6

4. C O U N C I L   B L U F F S
   7   8   9

5. I O W A   C I T Y
   10   11

6. W I L D   R O S E
   12   13

C R O S S   O F F
7 13 1 4 4   1 9 9

E F F I G Y   M O U N D S.
2 9 9 10 3 11   5 1 6 8 12 4

Cross off Effigy Mounds National Monument on page 30.

WHERE!
Amana Colonies

Iowa State Fair Butter Cow

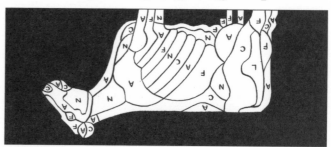

WHAT?

WHO?
Amelia Jenks Bloomer

The Crew

Editor: Andrew Gutelle
Writer: Lisa Feder-Feitel
Art Director: Jeff George
Illustrator: Frank Bolle
Map Illustrators: Andrew Shiff
                and Sherry Neidigh
Map Writer: Sally Issacs

Managing Editor: Margie Hayes
                Richmond
Copy Editor: Juanita Galuska
Graphic Assistant: David Justice

©1999 Highlights for Children, Inc.
P.O. Box 18201
Columbus, Ohio 43218-0201
www.whichwayusa.com

Published by

Highlights® for Children Inc.

P.O. Box 18201
Columbus, Ohio 43218-0201

Printed in the United States of America
For information on *Which Way USA?*, visit
www.whichwayusa.com or call 1-800-962-3661.

ISBN 0-87534-40-7
1240 - A